Stürtz REGIO

SALZKAMMERGUT

Text by
Doris Seitz

Photos by
Martin Siepmann

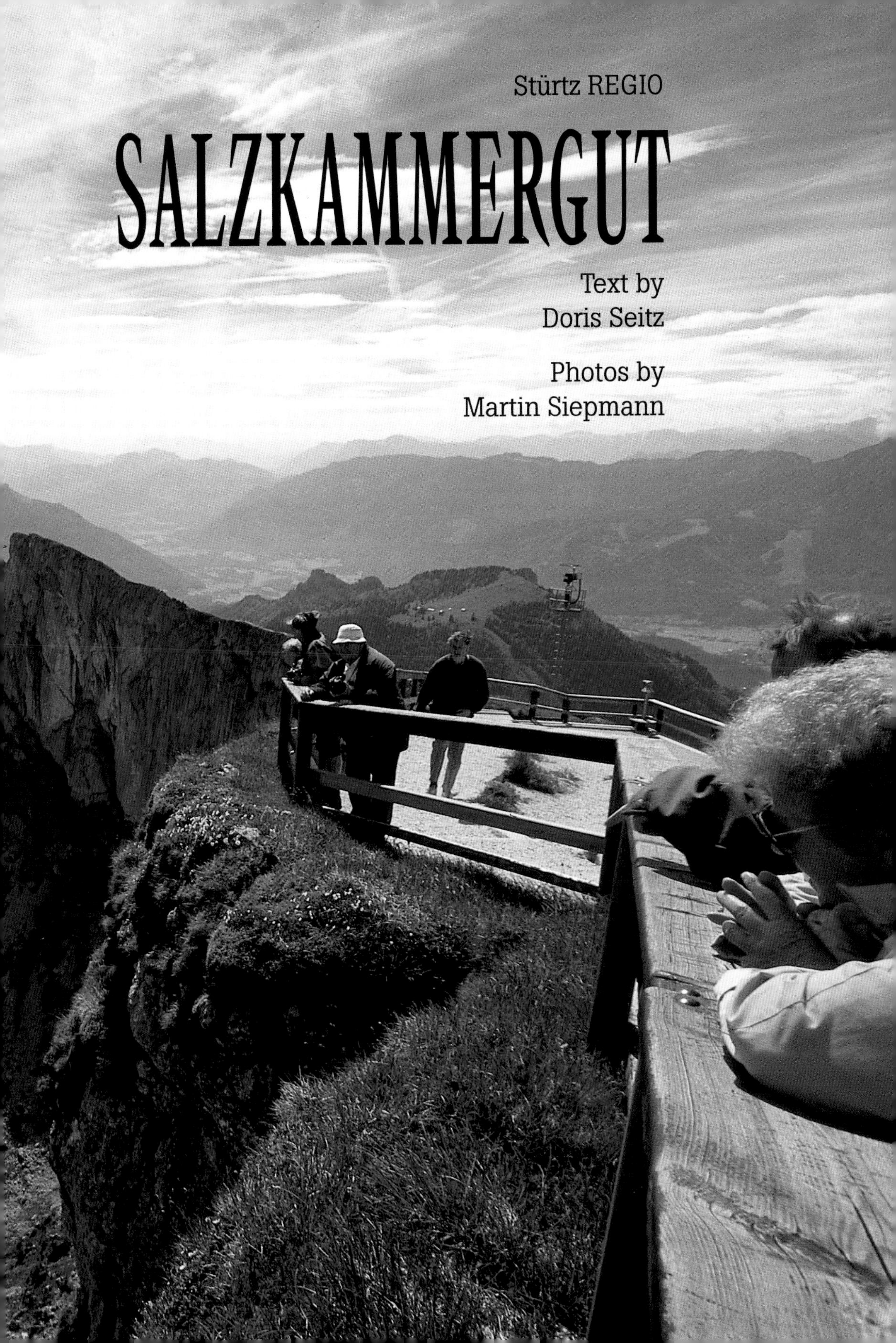

The Authors:

Doris Seitz was born in 1958. She studied journalism and now works as a freelance travel writer. She has written several travel guides. Her favoured topics include the various regions of Austria.

Martin Siepmann, born in Munich in 1962, is a freelance photographer. He has written numerous illustrated books on international and regional destinations. He has had reports and photographs printed in various travel magazines, including *Merian, GLOBO* and *GEO Saison,* and in books published by the World Wildlife Fund (WWF).

Credits

Photos:
Archiv für Kunst und Geschichte, Berlin:
p. 22 centre, p. 23 right, p. 28 bottom, p. 29 top, p. 51.
Stürtz Verlag archives: p. 23 left, p. 42, p. 50, p. 56 bottom.
Keltenmuseum Hallein, Hallein: p. 43 top.
We would like to thank Konditorei Zauner in Bad Ischl for allowing us to print the recipe on p. 35 and the following pictures: p. 34 left and p. 35 top.
The recipe on p. 57 was taken from *Österreich Küche, Land und Menschen* by Wolfgang Dähnhard and Peter Oberleither with the kind permission of Haedecke Verlag, Weil der Stadt.

Die Deutsche Bibliothek – CIP catalogue record
Salzkammergut / Martin Siepmann (photographer), Doris Seitz (author). –
Würzburg: Stürtz 1998.
ISBN 3–8003–1192–5 / paperback

Design: Förster Illustration & Grafik, Rimpar
Cartography: jf, Kartographie Jochen Fischer, Fürstenfeldbruck
Repro: Hofmüller, Linz
Translation: Ruth Chitty, Schweppenhausen
Printed and edited by the
Universitätsdruckerei H. Stürtz AG, Würzburg

ISBN 3–8003–1192–5 / paperback

*Top front cover:
St. Wolfgang.
Boats on the shore
of Lake Wolfgang.*

*Centre front cover:
cable car up
to the Katrinalm above
Bad Ischl.*

*Bottom front cover:
chic façades
characterise
St. Gilgen,
the main town in
the Salzburg part of
the Salzkammergut.
Bottom right:
the Kaiservilla in
Bad Ischl, Emperor
Franz Joseph I's
summer residence.*

*Back cover:
Hallstatt on
Lake Hallstatt.*

*Page 4/5: mountain
panorama looking
east from Schafberg
Mountain. To the left
down in the valley
is the Attersee.*

*Page 8/9: dawn
near St. Gilgen,
with views of
Lake Wolfgang
and Schafberg
Mountain.*

CONTENTS

A TREASURE ISLAND OF LAKES AND MOUNTAINS

"Austria consists of nine provinces and the Salzkammergut. The latter is made up of numerous salt mining communities *(Salzkammergüter)* which are like

miniature kingdoms without a king.

These communities are not exactly democracies – the Hapsburgs and other ruling dynasties are still too much part of everyday life for that – yet they are by no means dictatorships, for in these parts authority is something which is only considered important because everyone claims it for him- or herself."

Contemporary author Alfred Komarek, writing on the area in his book *Salzkammergut, Reise durch ein unbekanntes Land,* could hardly have put it better. To outsiders the Salzkammergut is a uniform whole; to those who live there it's a collective name for areas and communities whose shared characteristic is that they have nothing in common. It's precisely this independence, this originality and this contrast which lend this area of 37 by 37 miles of historical, cultivated land its charm – land which is actually an administrative nonentity. For almost three quarters of the region to the east of Salzburg belong to Upper Austria, with the rest shared by Styria and the Salzburger Land. Originally the word Salzkammergut, taken from a saltworks near Bad Ischl, was used to describe a small,

Grundlsee – which has the longest beach in the Salzkammergut – lies at the foot of the Totes Gebirge not far from Bad Aussee. Schloss Roth clings to its shores against a fantastic mountain backdrop.

very local area. It was later gradually extended to encompass a number of lakes, such as Traunsee, Grundlsee and Lake Hallstatt.

Further expansion of the Salzkammergut has been halted by geography. It confines the area to the east with the Totes Gebirge, a labyrinth of karst plateaux and mountain pastures, to the south with the glacier-capped, cave-riddled Dachstein group, to the

on a layer of schist cracked in two, forming today's Dachstein group and the Totes Gebirge. The primary rocks were covered with layers of chalk which rose and fell over the millennia. These also split, levelling the land with new paths, basins, grabens and valleys, through which underground rivers drove their course, shaping the main geographical features.

The Totes Gebirge (above) commands respect in the light of evening – seen from the lake, the mountains are overpowering.

The beautiful shores of Lake Fuschl. You can circle the lake on foot along easy, scenic paths in three hours.

southwest with the Tennengebirge, to the west with the broad basin of Lake Fuschl and to the north with the gentle slopes of Alpine foothills. The romantic area within its natural boundaries is a lacustrine paradise of around 80 lakes whose clear waters mirror the rugged peaks and sheer rock faces of the surrounding mountains, creating an image of serenity and still perfection.

Appearances, in this case, are deceptive. The Salzkammergut has never really been a haven of peace. Long before the Ice Age the earth here shook so violently that the huge limestone shelf which rested

A few million years later the Ice Age perfected the scenario,

producing glaciers and depressions which bored into the soft stone. When the ice melted thousands of years later the lakes remained, most of them fed by the Traun Glacier. The elements continue to mould these watery gems, among them Traunsee, Attersee, Mondsee and Irrsee, Lake Fuschl, Lake Wolfgang and Lake Hallstatt, Gosausee, Altausseer See, Grundlsee, Toplitzsee and Kammersee.

The lakes drew the first settlers to the area.

From 2800–1800 B.C. prehistoric dwellers on the Mondsee built their houses on stilts above the water level. It didn't take long for these early settlers to discover the treasure the Mesozoic Period had hidden in the bowels of the earth, a treasure which not only gave the region its name but also brought its inhabitants legendary wealth: salt. Technology developed and man started making methodical use of the area's natural resources and what he called his "white gold".

This "man in salt" belonged to the mysterious civilisation which had lived and worked in the Hallstatt salt mine between 800 and 400 B.C. The saline figure has since earned his place in the history books, as has his dwelling place.

Hallstatt became synonymous with an entire epoch,

the Hallstattian Age, famous all over the world. Yet until 1890 this enchanting little village on the fjord-like shores of Lake Hallstatt, where dark wooden chalets cling to the steep slopes like swallows' nests, could only be reached by ship or mule tracks.

This was an undertaking which was not without mishap, as the following story shows. In Hallstatt, which must be the oldest salt mine in the world, miners at work in 1734 came across a male body they thought recently dead. The unfortunate accident had, however, occurred more than two thousand years ago.

For centuries salt ruled the weal and woe of the people, incited historic battles for power, inspired technological advance and helped forge new avenues for trade and transport. In the early days salt was transported via land, later by river on salt barges and finally via special brine pipelines and, from 1836 onwards, horse tramway.

In 1839 the dainty steamer *Erzherzogin Sophie* undertook her maiden voyage from Gmunden to Ebensee, signalling the start of the Salzkammergut's grand era of shipping (which is still booming). In 1877 the first steam train puffed its way through the Salzkammergut from Attnang-Puchheim to Steinach-Irdning. After that there was no stopping the tourist trade.

The Salzkammergut was popular even before it mutated into a classic summer resort at the beginning of the 19th century. In 1797 researcher Alexander von Humboldt wrote to the director of the Botanical Gardens in Vienna, full of praise for the magnificent scenery: "I must admit that in Switzerland I don't know of any areas of natural beauty which are as splendid as those in Austria. And I find the people here are much more interesting and charming than the lethargic Swiss."

The Salzkammergut only really achieved world renown as a summer resort through the visits of long-term monarch Emperor Franz Joseph I, who spent 83 summers in Bad Ischl.

The little spa town still basks in the omnipresent imperial yellow

of its extravagant villas and palaces. Holidays surrounded by lakes and mountains were at first only fashionable with the nobility. Yet loyal subjects wanted to be where their sovereign was and soon began flocking to the town from all corners of the Hapsburg empire. More elite

Bad Ischl's magnificent spa rooms in the park are now an events and conference centre. This is where Ischl's Operettenwochen take place each year from July to September.

Grand villas (below) line the lakeside promenade of Gmunden on the Traunsee where the salt trade brought many citizens wealth and prosperity.

visitors included Archduke John, who discovered the Salzkammergut long before Emperor Franz Joseph I. In the Ausseer Land he met the love of his life, non-royal postmaster's daughter Anna Plochl, whom the emperor's son married in 1827

Elisabeth and her husband Carl Ferdinand spent many summers here, bringing with them the mute swans which make the idyll of the Traunsee complete. Even the Romans appreciated the tranquil qualities of the Salzkammergut's

Schloss Ort on the Toskana peninsula is linked to the island castle of Ort by a wooden bridge almost 430 feet long.

despite hefty opposition from all sides. The aristocracy also bequeathed some of its sparkle to Gmunden on Traunsee, where for years the Salt Authorities kept close tabs on trade from the Kammerhof.

Grand Duke Leopold II of Tuscany fled to Gmunden with his family.

In 1870 he had the Villa Toskana built here for his son on a peninsula near the island castle of Ort – the villa is now a congress centre. The royal house of Hanover also chose modest Gmunden as its place of summer residence, as did Princess Louise of Prussia. Archduchess

deepest lake, bestowing upon it the title *lacus felix*, happy lake.

It didn't take long for the artists to follow the well-to-do and the lords and ladies of the gentry. From the second half of the 19th century onwards, literati, intellectuals, painters and musicians discovered the almost fictitious beauty of the resort to be a rich source of inspiration. The restless traveller Friedrich Hebbel, for example, found not only his second home in Gmunden on the Traunsee but also inner peace: "In Upper Austria one has fallen under the curse or blessing of *dolce far niente* to such an extent that one must demonstrate true resolve to tear oneself away from the grips of leisurely thoughts aroused by the wealth of ever-changing impressions." In the summer months literary figures Gottfried Keller, Hugo von Hofmannsthal and Arthur Schnitzler and musicians Johannes Brahms, Hugo Wolf and artist Gustav Klimt could usually be found in Unterach on the Attersee with its multitude of fish. The king of the waltz, Johann Strauß, waved his baton at Ischl's Kurtheater in 1879 to a gala performance of *Die Fledermaus*. There were famous, illustrious individuals everywhere you looked.

The monarchy collapsed in 1918, yet the elegant and the rich continued to convene in Bad Ischl and Gmunden, carrying on with their effervescent and colourful mode of

the great and imperial, of art, patronage and the bohemian world. On the surface everything stayed the same, yet beneath it the inhabitants of the Salzkammergut began searching for new possibilities more in keeping with the times. They decided to refurbish the resort, transforming it into

a place of accomplished leisure, an artistic pendulum swaying between decadent laziness and spontaneous activity.

Their investment paid off, for their area with its abundance of lakes and mountains still attracts hoards of visitors from all over the globe. The region is also a favourite with

Schloss Hüttenstein on the Krotensee near St. Gilgen has been heavily restored (left).

life as before. Bad Ischl was ruled by operetta. Emmerich Kálmán, Oscar Strauß and Franz Lehár composed here to their heart's content.

The Second World War put an abrupt end to the Salzkammergut of

prominent politicians taking a break from the Bundestag, in particular German chancellor Helmut Kohl. For years he has shown holiday loyalty to St. Gilgen on Lake Wolfgang where Mozart's mother Anna Maria Pertl first saw the light of day in 1720.

From 1912 to his death in 1948 Franz Lehár lived in this villa in Bad Ischl (above). He wrote 24 of his operettas here.

An old pilgrimage route leads off from St. Gilgen past monuments shrouded in mystery

remain a puzzle to the art historian world. The most spectacular artefact inside the church is the high altar by Michael Pacher from South Tyrol.

It's not pilgrims but tourists who today flood to lively St. Wolfgang, which soared to fame in the 1930s thanks to the operetta "Im Weißen Rössl am Wolfgangsee" and is also something of

up to Falkenstein, where Wolfgang, the bishop of Regensburg, lived a life of recluse. He is said to have performed a wondrous deed. Legend has it that the hermit, tor-

Back from their excursions, the boats moor up for the night in Strobl on the shores of Lake Wolfgang. Away from its tourist bustle, Strobl has several extravagant villas and a fine Late Baroque parish church waiting to be discovered.

mented by the Devil, hurled his magic axe into the valley and swore that he would have Satan build a church at the place where he found it. A house of God was duly erected, and with it St. Wolfgang, place of pilgrimage *par excellence,* was founded.

The little chapel was soon bursting at the seams, so in 1429 a bigger church was erected in the village. Its irregular plan and unique form

an El Dorado for water-sports fans.

Zealous travellers ride up to the spectacular viewing platform atop Schafberg Mountain on the railway, in operation since August 1, 1893, to admire the entire Salzkammergut stretched out beneath them.

The Mondsee curves like a crescent moon beneath the steep slopes of the Drachenwand and Schafberg. It was here on the shores of the Salzkammergut's warmest lake that the first settlers built their homes, as you can see in the pile village museum. Just as impressive is the view down into the unfathomable depths on a cold, windless day, where with a bit of luck you might catch a glimpse of a sunken village in its watery grave. The Toplitzsee, which you pass on the romantic Three Lakes Tour from Grundlsee to the Kammersee waterfall, is also

said to hide things strange and mysterious. During the Nazi period fabulous riches and golden treasures were supposedly sunk here. Searches have indeed unearthed caskets of forged pound notes from the Third Reich. But the "treasure of the Alpine fortress" has yet to resurface... ▩

The rack railway (top left) in St. Wolfgang has been grinding up Schafberg Mountain since 1893.
The top of Schafberg Mountain (above), almost 6,000 feet above sea level, affords marvellous panoramic views of the Salzkammergut lakes, among them water-sports paradise Mondsee (bottom left).

Artists and intellectuals used to come in scores to the Attersee (main photo), the Salzkammergut's largest lake. One of their favourite places was Schloss Litzlberg (top left), surrounded by water, near Seewalchen (top centre).

Top right and centre:
the little house in Steinbach
where Gustav Mahler composed.
Above: concerts are staged on a
regular basis at Schloss Kammer
near Schörfling.

Mondsee (top left), situated on the northwest point of the lake of the same name, offers a broad range of leisure activities. Mondsee's music festival (Musiktage), for example, takes place in the first week of September each year.

Mondseer Rauchhaus
open-air museum
(main photo) is
southeast of
St. Michael's parish
church (left),
Mondsee's pride
and joy. The interior
was fashioned by
Swiss artist Meinrad
Guggenbichler,
who also created
the splendid Corpus
Christi Altar with
its rotund cherubs
(top right).

21

ROMANCE IN A MINOR KEY

The romance between Emperor Franz Joseph I and Elisabeth, Duchess of Bavaria, started like the beginning of a schmaltzy film. In 1853 the imperial family travelled to Bad Ischl for the summer where young Emperor Franz Joseph was to get engaged to his cousin Helene on August 18, his 23rd birthday. That, at least, was what his parents intended. Yet, as anyone who's seen the *Sissi* film trilogy (starring Romy Schneider and Karlheinz Böhm) knows, things didn't go according to plan.

Romy Schneider and Karlheinz Böhm in the role of the famous imperial couple (1955).

Their happiness at Bad Ischl's Kaiservilla (bottom; to the right the Red Salon) was sadly very short.

The entourage of Bavarian relations included the Wittelsbach princess's younger sister, Elisabeth — or Sisi, to spell her nickname cor-rectly — whom her mother Ludovika had brought along out of duty.

Franz Joseph fell head over heels in love with this pretty, carefree young lady

and a few days later — on the Emperor's birthday — their engagement was celebrated in Haus Austria on the Ischl esplanade, now the town museum.

After eight months of betrothal, Elisabeth, Duchess of Bavaria and a mere 16 years and four months old, married Franz Joseph, Emperor of Austria, in the Augustinerkirche in Vienna on April 24, 1854. Austria had gained an extremely popular, stunningly beautiful female monarch. The emperor's mother gave the young couple Villa Eltz as a wedding present which was henceforth known as the Kaiservilla. This imperial home is now a museum. The emperor's great-grandson and his family live in the left wing of the building.

What started so promisingly ended in tragedy.

Franz Joseph turned out to be a chronically overworked head of state; Elisabeth suffered at the hands of her mother-in-law who interfered with how she

brought up her four children; she also refused to observe ceremonial palace protocol in Vienna and felt her husband didn't understand her. And the emperor, who really did love her, had to admit that he couldn't fathom why she always had her "head in the clouds", to quote him. Sisi sought escape in her own world; she devoted herself to poetry, rode a lot and travelled widely. She developed a love for Hungary, a love the Hungarians reciprocated so passionately that in 1867 they crowned her their queen.

The liaison Franz Joseph had with kindred spirit Katharina Schratt – which went on for 30 years – began in 1883 with Sisi's consent, probably because she had a guilty conscience. With the actress Sisi felt her husband was in good hands; she was now free to travel for longer and longer periods. Sadly, it was this

which cost her her life. Whilst staying in Geneva, Empress Elisabeth was murdered by Italian anarchist Luigi Luccheni on September 10, 1898.

Sisi was married to Franz Joseph for 44 years. She only spent four of those years with her husband: so few for an *affaire du coeur* which had started so passionately in Bad Ischl. ▩

This is how Emperor Franz Joseph I (painted by Anton Einsle in c. 1848/50) liked his Sisi best: young, beautiful and carefree. This portrait of her by Franz Xaver Winterhalter from 1864 thus hung in the emperor's study.

Zwölferhorn Mountain above St. Gilgen on Lake Wolfgang, almost 5,000 feet high, is a glorious hiking spot with wonderful views and also a great place for experienced paragliders to practise.

Paragliding has also boomed in the Salzkammergut in these past few years. And who can blame the parapilots – what a wonderful way to see the Salzkammergut world of glittering lakes and dramatic mountain peaks.

25

A Mozart fountain was erected in honour of the great composer in 1927 in front of St. Gilgen's town hall.

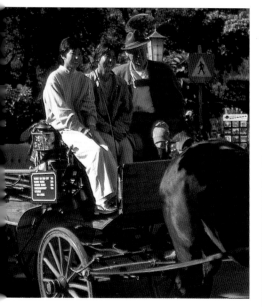

When in the Salzkammergut, a trip on a horse-and-cart is a must!

Mozart's mother was born in St. Gilgen. A commemorative plaque on the façade of the house she was born in (now a Mozart memorial, main photo) shows her and her daughter Nannerl (top).

"IM WEISSEN RÖSSL AM WOLFGANGSEE"

It was December 30, 1897, and a new star twinkled among the theatrical gods of Berlin. Dr. Oscar Blumenthal, director of the Lessing Theater, and actor Gustav Kadelburg had just premiered their three-act comedy "Im Weißen Rössl".

Their plot was based on a true story

which had taken place in the Weißes Rössl inn in Lauffen, a place of pilgrimage near Bad Ischl. Little did they suspect that their small-time stage triumph was to lay the foundations of international success for a later operetta: "Im Weißen Rössl am Wolf-gangsee".

Scene from a 1931 performance of "Im Weißen Rössl" at the Großes Schauspielhaus in Berlin.

It was none other than Ufa film star Emil Jannings (he of world acclaim) who extracted the play from his memory banks. He made his stage debut with a minor role in the play – incidentally now 100 years old – at the tender age of 16. At the pinnacle of his career in 1929, Jannings was sitting on one of the prettiest terraces on the shore of his new home, Lake Wolfgang, with a few colleagues and theatrical director Erik Charell. They were looking for a bright idea for a spirited revue they were planning for Berlin. Gazing out over the lake, Jannings spotted the Weißes Rössl inn and the merry farce he had debuted in came flooding back. The contents were simple and charming: hilarious scenes taken from the life of the pub's landlady, Josepha Vogelhuber, on the lookout for a husband, whom she finds in the form of her head waiter Leopold with the personal blessing of Emperor Franz Joseph. Jannings was able to convince his colleagues that the play was just what they were looking for.

The Weißes Rössl stayed white and the landlady smart, but the story was subject to poetic licence; it was moved from Lauffen in Traun Valley to Lake Wolfgang, whose sunny shores, wooded peaks and Schafberg Mountain offered a much friendlier backdrop for filming purposes. Ralph Benatzky wrote some suitably infectious music, Robert Stolz and Bruno Granichstaedten contributed a few songs and Robert Gilbert scripted the libretto.

and Johannes Heesters in 1952. The most popular film version of the tale is that brought out in 1960, however, with Peter Alexander, Waltraud Haas and Gunther Philipp.

The traditional hotel in St. Wolfgang still pulls the crowds. The Weißes Rössl and the town in general seem to personify what people throughout the globe commonly understand by the concept of Salzkammergut. ∎

Left: cover of the programme from the 1930 stage premiere in Berlin. Rudolf Forster, Johanna Matz and Walter Müller starred in the film "Im Weißen Rössl" in 1952.

The result was first performed in Berlin on November 8, 1930,

and was an immediate hit worldwide. It made idyllic St. Wolfgang on Lake Wolfgang and the inn, built in 1878, famous overnight. Soon the whole world discovered that people knew how to have a good time in the Salzkammergut.

With all this prominence it wasn't long before the play was filmed. Willi Forst produced a screen version starring Johanna Matz, Walter Müller

The Weißes Rössl Hotel on the lake shore in St. Wolfgang was built in 1878 and rose to fame as the place where the famous operetta took place. It's now a popular tourist attraction.

There are lots of ways to relax in St. Wolfgang (main photo). Why not take a trip on its beautiful lake – or just take time out over coffee and cake on the lakeside terrace of the Weißes Rössl Hotel (below)?

The famous white horse (weißes Rössl) dominates many a shop window in St. Wolfgang and is a popular motif for photographers of all denominations.

There are grand panoramic views of the Ischl Valley from the Katrinalm (top left). Below, on the northern banks of the Ischl River, lies Emperor Franz Joseph's summer residence (main photo). In the expansive grounds of the palace the emperor continues to pursue his favourite pastime: hunting (below). And on the Traun River St. Nepomuk keeps a protective eye on Bad Ischl (top right).

SEDUCTION IN SUGAR

No other has mastered the art of seduction in Bad Ischl as perfectly as the Zauners, a family of pastry cooks. The excellent reputation of the purveyors to the court has been upheld since 1832, when Johann Zauner first opened his cake shop on Pfarrgasse 7 at the instigation of Viennese medic Franz de Paula Wirer.

Zauner's remains t h e institution for the sweet tooth.

Bad Ischl has never had a "proper" Kaffeehaus. It never really needed one, for any-one who was someone just popped into Zauner's, whether their name was Johann Strauß, Franz Lehár, Johannes Brahms, Anton Bruckner or Katharina Schratt. In the back room café-goers played tarot or bridge. The salon on the first floor was reserved for the emperor. Tired aristocrats, industrialists and patrons of the arts came here to recover from their walks. Children dressed up like dolls obediently sat at the café tables with their governesses and gorged themselves on sweet delicacies fit for a king – or an Austrian emperor.

Zauner's Oblaten wafers, made according to the same traditional recipe since 1893, are absolutely delicious. The other titbits on display (right) are also enough to make your mouth water.

He was said to be particularly fond of *Ischler Törtchen, Zaunerkipferl* and *Zauner Stollen.*

Business at the cake shop and café continued to boom after the First World War and the fall of the monarchy, prompting Viktor Zauner to expand. In 1927 he opened a second café on the Traun River, the Café Zauner-Esplanade on Hasnerallee 2, which was as frequented as the original.

Holiday guests enjoyed coffee and cakes to salon music tinkling in the background.

In 1982 the café was restored to capture the style and atmosphere of Austria's "Kaiser und König" period and the café's technology brought up to date. During the high season in summer more than

80 people work here, 30 of them as pastry cooks. In the summer months *chef de cuisine* Josef Zauner produces over 200 kinds of fresh cake daily. Each one is a sugary delight; the mouth waters just to look at them.

The number of famous names have dwindled somewhat over the years, but the statutory meeting place in Bad Ischl is still "beim Zauner" for cake connoisseurs of all ages, couples on a rendezvous and people who want to see and be seen.

A few sets of distinguished taste buds Bad Ischl's confectioner *extraordinaire* has tickled in recent years are those of England's Queen Mother and her grandchildren. A letter sent to Zauner's in the old lady's fair hand, dated December 14, 1987, thanks them for the exquisite pastries Her Majesty received as a souvenir and which the royal palate savoured with great pleasure. ▪

Ischler Törtchen
(Ischl Bisquits)

Ingredients: For the shortcrust pastry: 300 g (11 oz) butter, 150 g (5 oz) icing sugar, 1 egg yolk, a pinch of salt and grated lemon rind, 450 g (1 lb) wheat flour
For the Ischl cream filling: Chocolate cream:1/4 l (1/2 pt) whipping cream, 80 g (3 oz) butter, 120 g (4 oz) sugar, 200 g (7 oz) plain chocolate; vanilla cream: 20 g (1 oz) vanilla cream mix, 2 egg yolks, 1/4 l (1/2 pt) milk, 50 g (2 oz) sugar.
As well: Apricot jam, chocolate fondant (for the glaze), chopped pistachios.

Cream the butter, sugar and spices. Quickly fold in the flour and leave the dough in the fridge for 2 hours. Then roll it out until it is 2 mm (1/10") thick and cut out biscuits using a round, 6 cm (2 1/2") pastry cutter. Bake on a tray in the oven at 170°C (325°F) until golden brown. Leave to cool.

For the Ischl cream filling: first make the chocolate cream by putting the whipping cream, butter and sugar into a saucepan and bringing to the boil. Remove the pan from the heat and whisk in the chocolate, chopped into small pieces, until it melts. Put the chocolate cream into a bowl and leave to cool down a little before placing in the fridge for 2 hours. Prepare the vanilla cream by mixing the cream mix and egg yolk with a little of the cold milk. Bring the remaining milk to the boil with the sugar, add the egg mixture and whisk until thick and creamy. Leave to cool in the fridge.

Take the stiff chocolate cream out of the fridge and allow it to reach room temperature. Stir the vanilla cream until smooth. Then beat the chocolate cream until frothy and mix with the vanilla. Stick two biscuits together with a thin, ca. 1 cm (1/2-inch) layer of the finished cream filling. Return the biscuits to the fridge to allow the cream to set. Then brush the biscuits with hot apricot jam, glaze with chocolate fondant and sprinkle with chopped pistachios for decoration.

Guten Appetit!

The village of Gosau (main photo) lies scattered in an isolated high mountain valley, popular for its lakes and the fantastic countryside man and beast feel at one with.

Gushing streams flow into the
Vorderer Gosausee (top right).
The Hinterer Gosausee can only
be reached on foot.

*With peaks topping almost
10,000 feet, the Dachstein
massif is a bizarre world of
rock and ice, as this
impressive view from the
Krippenstein demonstrates
(top left). Fjord-like
Lake Hallstatt (bottom left)
and the Vorderer Gosausee
(right) zigzag around
the foot of the Dachstein.*

The Catholic parish church dedicated to the Assumption of the Virgin Mary clings to the rock above the roofs of Hallstatt (right). Its most valuable exhibit is the Late Gothic high altar, one of the most beautiful in Upper Austria. The altar panels depict scenes from the life of the Madonna (below).

The charnel house in the cemetery chapel crypt contains around 1,200 skulls in neat rows, many of them bearing the names and dates of the deceased or decorative motifs.

With its idyllic setting and picture-book buildings, Hallstatt (main photo) has earned a reputation for itself as one of the most charming towns in the Salzkammergut. Together with Obertraun, Gosau, parts of Bad Goisern and the Dachstein plateau, Hallstatt was made a UNESCO World Heritage Site towards the end of 1997.

THE SEARCH FOR "WHITE GOLD"

Rome was an insignificant array of round huts when the first settlers in Hallstatt finally plucked up the courage to start mining deposits in their local salt mountain. In Jerusalem King David had just been superseded by wise judge Solomon, and in Greece the blind poet Homer had started writing his *Odyssey.*

Shipping salt in the days of yore: a barge carrying salt passes through the Traunfall lock. Drawing by Gustav Imlauer from c. 1840.

It was a quirk of geological history which enabled civilisations living in Hallstatt three thousand years ago to hack their way through the earth's crust to mine their "white gold", a cherished trade commodity which they transported by river on special wooden barges.

salt deposit remained which over the millennia were covered with impermeable layers of sandstone and clay. These deposits later provided the people of what has become known as the Hallstattian Age (800 – 400 B.C.) with their main source of wealth and spicy nourishment.

The salt deposits of the Salzkammergut were created a good 200 million years ago,

when a salty primeval sea flooded huge stretches of land of continental proportions. Lagoons were formed along the coasts, whose banks prevented the floods from draining away. The concentration of solutes gradually increased and the bays dried out. Disc-shaped areas of

The early mining communities of what is probably the oldest salt mine in the world had to labour hard with their simple implements before they were rewarded with blocks of pure salt. Finds from the Hallstattian Age show that salt had to be strenuously hewn from the rock using wooden pickaxes and other hand tools.

It is thought that salt mining ceased during the Roman period. It flour-

Brine being evaporated to salt in a huge pan. In 1757/58 Benedict Werkstätter executed an entire cycle of paintings on salt extraction.

ished again in the 13th century, however, in Hallstatt, Bad Ischl and Altaussee. It was at this time that medieval man hit upon the idea of drawing salt from the rock with the help of water. From this point forward the salt layers were leached using increasingly modern techniques. The water, saturated to brine, was either evaporated at the Ebensee saltworks to produce table salt (in Hallstatt alone ca. 200,000 metric tons of salt are extracted every year) or used for

have children was as yet unmet. Her longing for offspring was finally fulfilled in 1830. After two miscarriages she presented the House of Hapsburg with a royal heir who later became Emperor Franz Joseph I. In 1832 she gave birth to Ferdinand Maximilian and a year later to Karl Ludwig. The archduchess insisted

healing purposes, such as in Ischl in 1823. It was around then that the sleepy little village grew into a chic spa, thanks to Viennese doctor Franz de Paula Wirer (1771–1844).

His first patients included Archduchess Sophie, whose desire to

on ascribing her welcome fertility to the healing powers of Ischl's brine spa, upon which history christened her three sons the Salt Princes. ■

A trip through the bizarre underworld of the salt mine at Bad Ischl is something of an adventure for young and old.

In the Salzkammergut customs are governed by the church year and not by the various calendars of events organised by local tourist offices. Corpus Christi, for example, sees the staging of lavish processions in the towns and villages. This religious holiday is celebrated in a particularly spectacular manner in Hallstatt, when worshippers take to the waters of Lake Hallstatt in boats.

Corpus Christi processions have taken place on the lake in Hallstatt since the 17th century – providing the weather is good.
The tradition of lake parades came about because the narrow promontory was heavily populated and space on land thus rather limited.

Wooden houses with decorative porches and balconies characterise the little spa town of Altaussee (right), which, like its neighbour Bad Aussee (below), thrived on its salt mines in centuries past.

*After Spring has liberally
carpeted the meadows with
white, star-shaped narcissi,
the Ausseer Land celebrates
the blooms at the end of
May/beginning of June
with a festival parade on
land and water.*

6,030–foot Loser Mountain in the Ausseer Land is a popular place for outings (top right). Safe steps cut into the rock pass a window in the mountain (the Loserfenster, left) on their way to the summit. There are spectacular views from the Loserstraße (bottom right), which winds from Altaussee up to the restaurant on the mountain.

A GRAND SOURCE OF INSPIRATION

Adalbert Stifter painted this oil of the Altausseer See with the Sarstein in the background in 1835 (Vienna, Historisches Museum).

"...[and] so I found the place where I would permanently settle, that valley in the Styrian mountains, and this stretch of country became my friend, as a person becomes a friend after years of trial and experience..." Writer Jakob Wassermann found these words to praise his chosen home of Altaussee, of which he also wrote (in a less magnanimous mood): "Altaussee is not a village but an illness one cannot be rid of."

Jakob Wassermann was not alone; many artists, actors, composers, intellectuals, poets and thinkers from the *fin de siècle* to the present day have nurtured an empathy with Altaussee. The magical beauty of the resort has attracted a whole host of spirits,

as if the Salzkammergut were a paradise

tailored to meet their requirements. Whether on the Attersee, Traunsee or Mondsee, on Lake Wolfgang, Grundlsee or Altausseer See, each has found his or her own place of refuge and inner peace.

The poet Baron Joseph Christian von Zedlitz, a friend of Joseph von Eichendorff's and Franz Grillparzer's, was probably the first to set up home in Altaussee "out of love for nature and for the charm of this wonderful area". He bought up land on the Altausseer See in 1847 and built the Seehaus, which rapidly became a popular meeting place for poets such as Nikolaus Lenau, Adalbert Stifter and Franz Grillparzer and for scientists and members of the nobility.

Altaussee soon became a talking point, drawing a number of curious individuals. In 1864 Imperial Chancellor Hohenlohe's family settled here; not long afterwards grand villas began springing up everywhere to house the well-endowed. In 1896 *Simplicissimus* magazine printed the story *Das Dorf im Gebirge* about a village in the mountains (Altaussee), penned by Hugo von Hofmannsthal and edited by Jakob Wassermann. Jung-Wien followed in Hofmannsthal's wake, a circle of young wordsmiths which included Arthur Schnitzler, Raoul Auernheimer, Hermann Bahr and Leopold von Andrian-Werburg. The latter's father already owned a property on the lake, the Andrian Villa, which was henceforth turned into one of the literary summer salons typical of the time.

The list of famous honorary Altausseer is endless.

Actor Klaus Maria Brandauer and writer Barbara Frischmuth still reside here. You encounter many names along the Via Artis, three self-contained art routes which weave past 14 historic buildings where great minds once thought, wrote, painted and composed. ■

Jakob Wassermann, born in Central Franconia in Germany, spent many years of his life in Altaussee, his chosen second home.

…In June the people from the city have arrived and taken up residence in all the large rooms. The farmers and their wives sleep in the attic full of old horse tack, full of dusty sledge harnesses with jangling, little yellow bells, full of old winter jackets, old flintlocks and rusty, misshapen saws. They have carried all their things out of the lower rooms and cleared out all their trunks for the people from the city; nothing remains in these rooms except the smell of the dairy in the cellar and of old wood, which in invisible pillars seeps out of the interior of the house through small windows, sour and cool, wafting over the heads of the pale red hollyhocks to the huge apple trees.
Only the decoration on the walls has been left as it is: sets of antlers and the many small pictures of the Virgin Mary and the saints in gilded and paper frames, with rosaries made from false corals or tiny wooden beads interspersed between them. The women from the city hang their large garden hats and their coloured parasols on the antlers…

(from: Hugo von Hofmannsthal, Das Dorf im Gebirge)

First stop on the Three Lakes Tour of the Grundlsee
(top right), Toplitzsee and Kammersee –
well worth undertaking for the rewarding view
of the countryside – is Gößl (bottom right)
at the southwest end of the Grundlsee.
It's a 20-minute walk from here to the mysterious
Toplitzsee (left), where the journey is continued
by motor boat to the smaller Kammersee.

Winter on the idyllic
Almsee, stretched out
beneath the steep, rocky
inclines of the Totes
Gebirge (top three photos).
The Glöcknerlauf
procession in Ebensee
also commands attention
with its colourful
display of local culture
(bottom left).

The view from the
Feuerkogel of the sea
of cloud hanging over
the Traunsee and out
towards Traunstein
and the Hochkogel is a
particularly impressive
natural spectacle
(main photo).

FISH IN DRINKING WATER

Perch, pike and trout (below) thrive in the clear lakes of the Salzkammergut. Why not try one of the delicious fish dishes at one of the region's fish restaurants (right)?

Hallstattian caviar, slices of Mondsee pike, fillets of Attersee char, Lake Wolfgang whitefish "nach Müllerin Art", Grundlsee fish ragout, chargrilled Traunsee fish kebab: local menus keep their piscatorial promises, and there are plenty of them lurking in the waters of the Salzkammergut. Smoked, fried or au bleu, simply prepared or served *à la nouvelle cuisine,* there's something for everyone who likes fish.

The multitude of fish in the Salzkammergut is legendary.

Most places on the Mediterranean can only dream of such variety. Over 30 different species, the majority of them char, trout and whitefish, happily wriggle their way through the totally clear waters of the region. Local pubs and restaurants are proud to advertise their fish as those that "swim in drinking water".

There seems to be some truth behind this sales claim that the silent, slippery treasures of the Salzkammergut are of high quality. During Austria's regency period, fish from the area were considered a special delicacy and were transported live in wooden barrels to Vienna so that the emperor could enjoy fresh fish at his table. This quality was (and still is) guaranteed by the fact that for several centuries

fishing in the Salzkammergut has been subject to strict regulations. The lakes belong to the National Austrian Forestry Commission, for example. The fish are the private property of those professional

fishermen who have bought up a percentage of the rights to the lake.

Fishing, which started in the Salzkammergut in the 12th century, is today practised by most professionals as a second occupation. On average a fisherman catches around 2,200 pounds of fish per season; the money he gets from sale of the fish is no longer enough to feed a family.

Sport fishing, on the other hand, is becoming increasingly fashionable.

Rigid bylaws also apply here, such as only fishing with humane methods and only from July 15 to September 1. In order to prevent the number of fish from diminishing unnecessarily, char under a foot and trout under 1'6" have to be thrown straight back into the water.

The fish population in the Salzkammergut is being decimated from within without external, human help. In the past two years, for example, the number of perch has drastically increased; one of their

foibles is that they eat young char. Still, anglers don't need to worry that there are no heavyweights to be had. Champion catches, such as the preserved, 57-pound trout on display at Grundlsee's administrative offices, are not an everyday occurrence, but possible. Carry on fishing! ▧

Whether on the Traunsee (left) or the Mondsee, fishing has been relegated to a second occupation – or just a sport.

Rainbow Trout in a Salt Crust

2 rainbow trout (each weighing 400g/14 oz), 1 lemon, pepper, 50 g (2 oz) fresh herbs, 2 kg (4 lbs) coarse sea salt, 2 egg whites, 3/8 l (5/8 pt) water, oil

Rinse the cleaned fish under cold, running water. Season the abdomen with pepper and lemon juice and stuff with the fresh herbs.

Fold strips of kitchen foil to the size of each fish and place on an oiled baking tray. Mix the sea salt with the egg whites and water to form a paste, then leave to stand for 5 minutes. Brush 1/3 of the salt paste into the foil fish moulds, place the trout on their moulds and brush the remaining paste over the fish in an even layer. Bake in the oven at 220°C (425°F) for 15 minutes.

Recommended wine:
Grüner Veltliner Smaragd (Spätlese) from the Wachau

Recipe by Christian Obermayr from the Marienbrücke restaurant in Gmunden. The restaurant serves ambitious (piscine) cuisine on the banks of the Traun. (An der Marienbrücke 5, A-4810 Gmunden. Tel.: +43-(0) 76 12-40 11)

Gmunden lies at the northernmost tip of the Traunsee. The prize possession of its parish church (Mariä Himmelfahrt) is the high altar with the Three Kings (right), carved by Thomas Schwanthaler in 1678. The town hall boasts a ceramic carillon from the 18th century (below).

Schloss Ort inhabits a small island in the Traunsee. The wings of the castle enclose an attractive courtyard framed with arcades (bottom left). There is a good view of Gmunden from the castle (main photo).

Traunkirchen, elegantly poised on a peninsula on the western shores of the Traunsee, is crowned by the Chapel of St. John on a rock spur up above it (main photo). The town's most remarkable artistic jewel is the fishermen's pulpit from 1753 in the Baroque parish church dedicated to the Virgin Mary (bottom right).

One of the sights
of Altmünster, the
oldest town on the
Traunsee, is its
17th-century
Schloss Ebenzweier
(left). Below:
Pension Schlößl
in Altmünster –
a room with a
view of the lake.

Following double
spread: in the
snows of winter,
when a thick cloud
of mist rises from
the lake, Schloss Ort
disappears into the
fog like a lost dream.

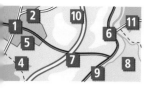

AT A GLANCE

An impressive sight: the Dachstein caves. Top right: there's a fantastic view of the lake from the terrace of Hotel Fuschl.

The state rooms at the Kaiservilla in Bad Ischl are opulent and elegant – here, the Red Salon.

1 Dachstein Caves

The three caves in Dachstein Mountain (Rieseneishöhle, Mammuthöhle and Koppenbrüllerhöhle) are **bizarre ice palaces** in a gigantic natural scenario. *(Rieseneishöhle and Mammuthöhle open May – Oct., Koppenbrüllerhöhle May – Sep. and by arrangement. Tel:. +43-(0)61 31-3 62)*

2 Fischerhütte Restaurant

Restaurateur **Albrecht Syen** has been serving fresh trout, freshwater char, pike, burbot, chub and **typical Styrian delicacies** at his rustic restaurant (also a snack bar) near the lake since 1975. *(Fischerhütte am Toplitzsee, Grundlsee. Open Dec. – Oct. Closed Wed. Tel.: +43-(0)36 22-82 96)*

3 Gmunden on the Traunsee

Gmunden, once seat of the Salt Authorities, is now a yearly meeting place for Austria's potters. **Splendid houses** bear witness to the town's wealthy past. The **town museum (Stadtmuseum)** in the Kammerhof with its Hebbel and Brahms Room is well worth a visit, as is the **island castle of Ort.** *(Stadtmuseum, Kammerhofgasse 8. Open May – Oct. Tues. – Sat. 10 a.m. – 12 p.m. & 2 – 5 p.m. Tel.: +43-(0)76 12-79 42 44)*

4 Hotel Schloss Fuschl

The **list of the hotel's distinguished guests** ranges from Prince Rainier of Monaco to Richard Nixon to Billy Wilder. The **luxury hotel and beauty farm** on a peninsula on Lake Fuschl used to be the Salzburg archbishops' hunting lodge and provided the setting for the *Sissi* films

in the 1950s. Here you can wine, dine and reside like royalty. For those with high expectations – and high salaries. *(Hof near Salzburg. Tel.: +43-(0)62 29-22 53-0)*

5 Kaiservilla and Park

Emperor Franz Joseph's **former summer residence** – where he signed the manifesto "To My Peoples" in 1914 – is now a **museum with numerous hunting trophies.** The Kaiservilla was a wedding present from Archduchess Sophie. *(Bad Ischl. Open daily May – Oct. 9 – 11.45 a.m. & 1 – 4.45 p.m. Rest of the year weekends only. Tel.: +43-(0)61 32-2 32 41)*

6 Café and Cake Shop Zauner

Since the café's opening in 1823, the former purveyors to the royal court can boast a number of **famous clients,** among them Emperor Franz Joseph, Bismarck, Franz Lehár and Shirley MacLaine. Zauner's extensive buffet offers delicious morsels to suit every palate, whereby their **Zauner Stollen** has earned the cake shop an acclaim which reaches far beyond local boundaries. *(Bad Ischl, Pfarrgasse 7. Tel.: +43-(0)61 32-2 35 22)*

7 Steinberghaus Arts Centre

Go to the museum of local history and literature, opened in 1994, to find out about the **Aussee art world.** Many writers, painters and musicians have been inspired by the Ausseer Land. Buried under the museum is **Altaussee's museum mine.**

(Altaussee, ca. 1 1/2 miles from the town centre. Open Jul. – Sep. 10 a.m.– 4 p.m. Tel.: +43-(0)36 22-7 16 43)

8 Lehár-Villa

Hardly anything has been changed since **composer Franz Lehár's** period of residence (1912 to 1948) in the villa where he wrote 24 of his operettas.

(Bad Ischl, diagonally opposite the Stadtmuseum.
Open daily over Easter & May – Sep. 9 a.m. – 12 p.m. & 2 – 5 p.m. Tel.: +43-(0)61 32-2 69 92)

9 St. Michael's in Mondsee

The oldest monastery in Austria, dissolved in 1791 and now privately owned, was the **cultural heart** of the region for over 1,000 years. The main attraction is the former collegiate church and now the Parish Church of St. Michael's, built in Late Gothic style between 1470 and 1487. Don't miss Swiss artist Meinrad Guggenbichler's **Corpus Christi Altar** in the left aisle.

10 Bad Dürrnberg Salt Mine

Embark on an underground journey in the **oldest salt mine in the world** back to the first millennium B.C. On your hour-long trip you will pass Celtic pinewood spills, mining chutes and a mysterious **salt lake.**

(Hallstatt, Salzbergstraße 21. Open Apr. – Oct. Tel.: +43-(0)61 34-82 51-72)

11 St. Wolfgang on Lake Wolfgang

The pub **Weißes Rössl,** commandeered by the Romantikhotel group in 1977, rose to fame in the 1930s through the operetta of the same name. Another crowd-puller is the 15th-century **Pacher Altar** in St. Wolfgang's local church. For an uplifting **view** of the world travel up to the top of Schafberg Mountain by rack railway.

(St. Wolfgang.
Tel.: +43-(0)61 38-23 06-0)

12 Stadtmuseum Bad Ischl

The young emperor Franz Joseph I got engaged to Elisabeth von Wittelsbach in **Haus Austria** in 1853. Full of historical paraphernalia, the building is now the town museum, offering facts and figures on local folklore, **salt mining** and **shipping on the Traun River.**

(Bad Ischl, Esplanade 10.
Open Apr. – Oct. Tue., Thur., Fri., Sat. & Sun. 10 a.m. – 5 p.m., Wed. 2 – 7 p.m. Closed Mon. (except Jul. & Aug.)
Open Jan. – Mar. Fri., Sat. & Sun. 10 a.m. – 5 p.m. Tel.: +43-(0)61 32-2 54 76)

13 Tourist Information

Further information is available from Ferienregion Salzkammergut, Wirer Straße 10, A–4820 Bad Ischl. Tel.: +43-(0)61 32-2 69 09-0.

Salzkammergut highlights: the Weißes Rössl (top), the rack railway on Schafberg Mountain, the Lehár Villa in Bad Ischl (top left) and the Corpus Christi Altar at St. Michael's in Mondsee (bottom left).

The numbers 1 – 13 refer to positions marked on the map on pages 2 and 3.

CHRONOLOGICAL TABLE

5000–1900 B.C. The first inhabitants settle in the Salzkammergut during the Neolithic Age. They live as hunters and gatherers in the high-lying valleys or dwell in pile villages in the valleys.

Striking country in the Ausseer Land: view of Loser Mountain and the Loseralm.

1800–900 B.C. Illyrian peoples (the Noricans) move into the area during the Bronze Age. They get as far as Hallstatt, where they are probably the first to mine salt.

800–400 B.C. Celtic Tauriscans settle in Hallstatt in around 800 B.C. Through local salt mining the settlement experiences an economic and cultural boom which lasts 400 years.

The Early Gothic spital church in Bad Aussee has two interesting winged altars from the 15th century. The high altar from 1449 was donated by Emperor Frederick III.

This period is known all over the world as the Hallstattian Age.

15 B.C. The Romans annex Noricum, the kingdom of the Celts, and start building the Roman Road (Römerstraße).

5th century A.D. The Romans leave and are replaced by Slavs who settle along the Römerstraße.

6th century Bavarian settlers come to the area and with them the first Christian missionaries. Monasteries, churches, castles, market towns and villages are built. The "Kammergut" is put under compulsory state control. A period of heavy oppression begins.

1260 Ottokar of Bohemia is crowned king. Aussee's salt mine makes up one twelfth of Styria's provincial income.

1309 Aussee is made a market town.

Bad Aussee is a popular holiday and spa resort with a Glauber salt spring and salt-water baths.

1460 The saltworks come under state ownership and several salt chambers *(Salzkammer)* are formed. Exploitation of the miners lasts for centuries.

1525 The Peasant Wars start, lasting for over 100 years. Those not killed by war fall victim to the plague, which rages in various areas.

1562 Ischl gains its own salt mine near Perneck.

1595 Emperor Rudolph II orders a brine pipeline to be built from Hallstatt to Ebensee via Ischl.

1805 As a result of the Napoleonic Wars there are 2,000 French troops in Aussee and 1,000 in the surrounding area.

1808 Archduke John becomes the protector of the region.

1834–1836 The horse tramway from Budweis to Linz is extended to the Salzkammergut in Upper Austria, considerably easing the transportation of salt. The horse tramway is taken out of service in 1856.

1848–1914 Emperor Franz Joseph I makes Ischl his summer residence. The imperial entourage draws the aristocracy and the more elevated members of society to the Salzkammergut.

23 October 1877 The first train puffs along the new Salzkammergut line.

Post–1918 The monarchy is no more, but elegance lives on in the Salzkammergut. Musicians, writers and artists flood to the region, still extremely popular with holidaymakers.

1938 German troops march into Austria.

1955 The Austrian Treaty of Independence is signed and the Second Republic founded.

1997 The Salzkammergut is still profiting from its splendid past but, due to the tense economic situation in Europe as a whole, is fighting a rapid decline in the number of tourists.

Part and parcel of any self-respecting health resort: the pump room in Bad Ischl, Austria's oldest salt-water spa.

The Zwölferhorn cable car from St. Gilgen whisks hikers and nature-lovers up the ca. 5,000 feet of Zwölferhorn Mountain in just 15 minutes. 10 minutes on foot and you're at the cross on the summit.

INDEX

SALZKAMMERGUT

OBERÖSTERREIC.

Lengau
147
Straßwalchen

Seeham
Nußdorf
Mattsee
Köstendorf
Neumarkt
Oberndorf
Obertrum
1
154
Laufen
156
F l a c h g a u
Zell
20
Henndorf
Saaldorf
Elixhausen
Seekirchen
Mondsee
9

Freilassing
A1
Plainfeld
Thalgau
151
304
1
St. Lorenz
158
Hof
Fuschl
154

D
Salzburg
Ebenau
Scharfling
20
Faistenau
4
Piding
1
St. Gilgen
8
150
Glasenbach
21
Grödig
Hinter-see
Großgmein
Hintersee
Abers

Adnet
allein
Vigaun
A
Hoher Zinken
▲
1764m
Pernegg
SALZBURG
Kuchl
A10
Golling
Scheffau
am Tennengebirge
159
Abtenau
TENNENGEBIRGE
Naturschutz-gebiet
0   5
© Kartographie Jochen F.